ARTOONS

ARTOONS

The Hystery of Art

Kevin Reeves

Kevin Reeves

Sound and Vision

Canadian Cataloguing in Publication Data
Reeves, Kevin, 1958-

ARTOONS, The Hystery of Art

Canadian Cataloguing in Publication Data

Reeves, Kevin, 1958-
Artoons, the hystery of art

ISBN 0-920151-05-1

1. Art – Caricatures and cartoons.
2. Art – Anecdotes, facetiae, satire, etc.
1. Title.

N7470.R44 1985   700'.2'07   C85-099557-4

Published in Canada by
SOUND AND VISION,
84 Bleecker Street,
Toronto M4X 1L8.

First Printing, October 1985.

ACKNOWLEDGEMENTS

I would like to thank everyone I pestered for opinions, especially the clan of 880 Bathurst St. Also, Greg Furmanczyk, Michael Wainwright, Frans Donker, and those whom I've forgotten to list due to my insufferable negligence. However, I will never forget the names of Mort Drucker and Johnny Hart, my childhood idols and unwitting mentors of tormenting wit.

Finally, to the artists who are represented in this book — for the pigments of their imaginations.

UNGER

"Blast, my pen keeps running out."

I knew Kevin Reeves when he was a human being. A
young schoolboy came to my home one day a few years back
and shyly showed me his drawings.
What do you do when you're a world-famous cartoonist and
a kid shows up at the door with drawings that are
better than yours?   I told him to join the army.
Well, I guess it was fortunate for everyone else that
he didn't take my advice. He has developed a fine talent,
laced with humour and an obvious affection for great
painters, past and present.
I am sure that Goya, Cezanne and Monet would have
enjoyed Kevin's work as much as I have.
The little frogs, sitting on lilly-pads, singing,
'We're in the Monet' is one of the funniest cartoons
I have seen in a long time.
I still think he should have joined the army.

Jim Unger

DEDICATION

To my parents, for letting me take my first can of spray paint into the gallery.

VAN EYCK'S MISCONCEPTION

GAUGUIN

JACOB WRESTLING WITH THE ANGEL

POINTILLISM

DA VINCI

"All this talk about pollution affecting Italian painting is ridiculous . . . in fact, it cracks me up."

DUCHAMP

BLAKE

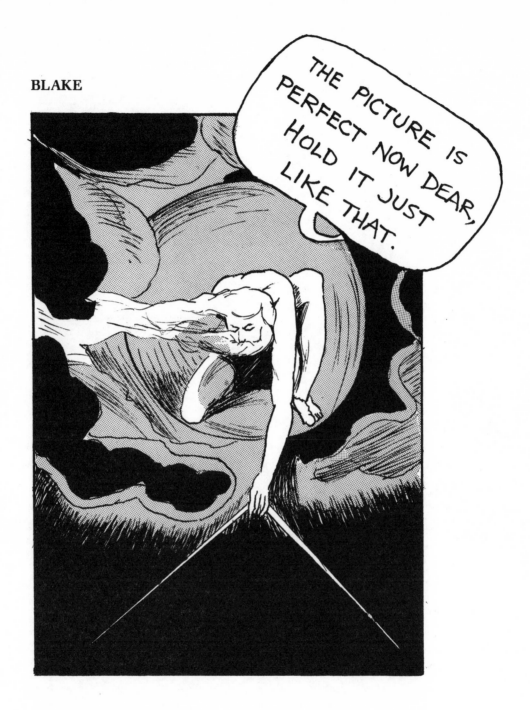

POLLOCK

"Oh no . . . not spaghetti AGAIN!"

MICHELANGELO

SUSPENDED ANIMATION

WHISTLER

"Thanks Mom."

DELACROIX

GARDEN PATH

CENSORING ART

GAINSBOROUGH

"Go blow your own horn — I am NOT Little Boy Blue!"

MONDRIAN

"Something tells me we're just under the Hague now."

DALI

"These Jane Fonda workouts are becoming ... more ... strenuous!"

DAVID

BONAPARTE CROSSING THE ALPS
(With apologies to Walt Kelly)

TITIAN

VAN GOGH

YOUNG HENRY MOORE

BEARDSLEY

DRISTAN
AND
ISOLDE

BATEMAN

GENTEEL PENGUINS AND WHALEBONES

GOYA

TOM THOMSON PAINTED WITH INTENT

HAUSSMANN

JOHANN SEBASTIAN BACH

"That damn Christo has been here."

PARMIGIANINO

MADONNA WITH THE LONG NECK

DUCHAMP

NUDE DESCENDING A STAIRCASE

CEZANNE

THE CARD PLAYERS

INGRES

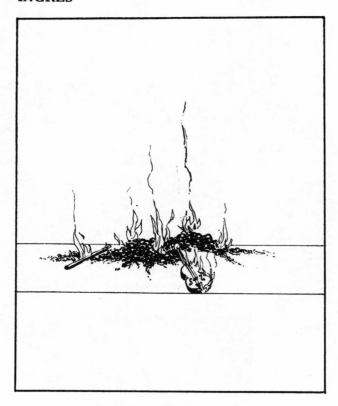

PORTRAIT OF PAGANINI

DAVID

OATH OF THE HORATII

DEGAS

MANET

CARAVAGGIO

"Darn trap didn't work!"

"I notice Michelangelo's 'Moses' has arrived."

DAVID

MADAME JULIE RECAMIER

BOTTICELLI

"He seems to be showing signs of improvement."

BRUEGEL

PEASANT UNDER GLASS

STEEN

SELF PORTRAIT

DALI

THAT SYNCHING FEELING

KLEE PIGEON SHOOTING

PICASSO

MAGRITTE

CLICK

"It's getting dark Sam . . .

will you turn on the light?

DEGAS/MANET

BALLERINAS PRACTISING AT THE BARRE

REMBRANDT

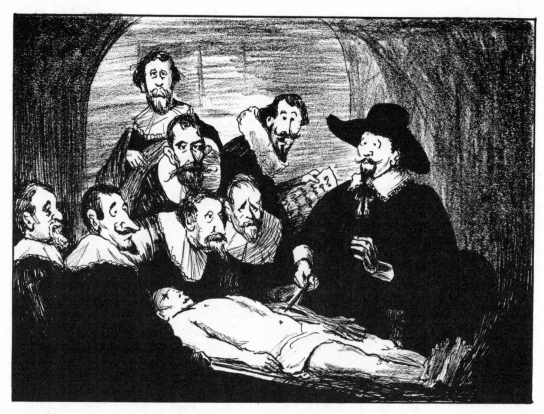

"Cadaver? I though you said caterer ... The cadaver doesn't come until Tuesday."

ROTHKO (DETAIL)

DAUMIER

DON QUIXOTE ATTACKING THE WINDMILL

EL GRECO

VIEW OF TOLEDO

"What do you get when you cross

Tououse — Lautrec and Andy Warhol?"

THE CAN - CAN - CAN

DA VINCI

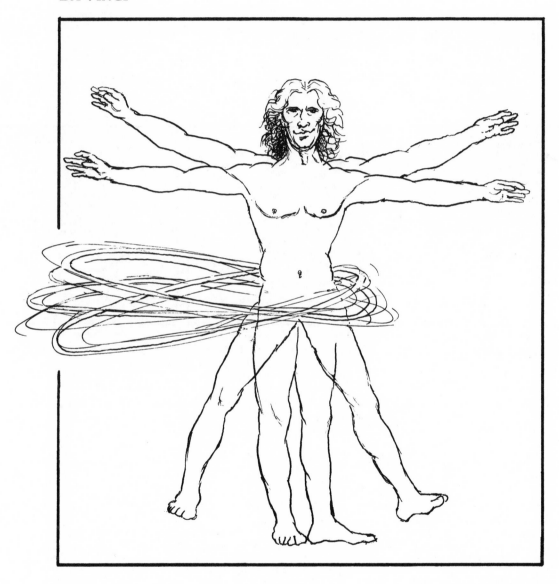

WATER LILIES

KLINE

O'KEEFFE

CHAGALL

"When you said, 'Let's go for a Float', I thought you meant chocolate."

DA VINCI

LAST SUPPER

RENOIR

THE LIGHTER SIDE OF IMPRESSIONISM

AN HYPOTHETICAL CARTOON

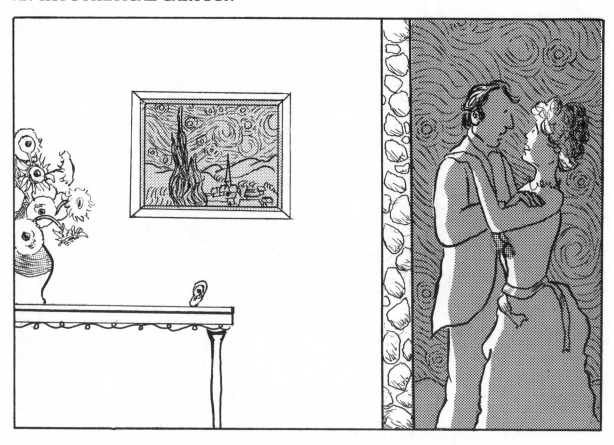

"No more Hans . . . Daddy likes to keep an ear out."

CARAVAGGIO

"Oh no, not split ends AGAIN!"

MILLET

ROUSSEAU

REED BETWEEN THE LIONS

REMBRANDT

. . . THOUGHT TO HAVE BEEN THE LAST . . .

. . . UNTIL THIS WAS DISCOVERED . . .

. . . HOWEVER . . .

HOLBEIN

WOOD

DANBY

TURNER

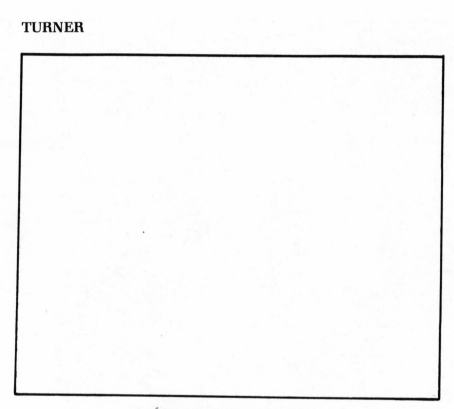

SNOW, WIND AND FOG

FUSELI

VERMEER

CALDER

MOBILE HOMES

BOTTICELLI

SHELL OIL

THE ATTEMPTED SUICIDE OF JEAN-PAUL RIOPELLE

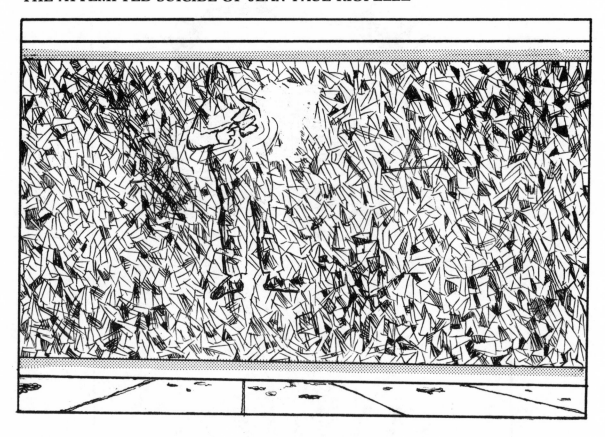

RODIN

COLVILLE

TURNER

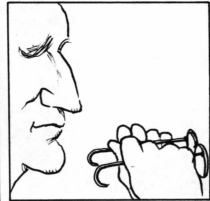

GERICAULT

CORREGGIO

CALLING OF ST. MATTHEW

SEURAT

SATYRICAL ART

CHRONOLOGY

VAN EYCK, Jan (1370-1426), *Flemish*

BOTTICELLI, Sandro (1444-1510), *Italian.*

DA VINCI, Leonardo (1452-1519), *Italian.*

MICHELANGELO, (Michelagniolo di Lodovico Buonarroti Simoni (1475-1565), *Italian.*

TITIAN, Tiziano Vecellio (1490-1576), *Italian.*

CORREGGIO, (Antonio Allegri) (1494-1534), *Italian.*

HOLBEIN THE YOUNGER, Hans (1497-1543), *German.*

PARMIGIANINO, Francesco Maria Mazzola, (1503-1540), *Italian.*

BRUEGEL, Pieter (c. 1526-1569), *Flemish.*

EL GRECO, Domenico Theotocopuli (1541-1614), *Greek.*

CARAVAGGIO, Michelangelo Merisi da (c. 1569-1609), *Italian.*

REMBRANDT, (Rembrandt van Rijn (1606-1669), *Dutch.*

STEEN, Jan (1626-1679), *Dutch.*

VERMEER, Jan (1632-1675), *Dutch.*

HAUSSMANN, Elias Gottlieb (1695-1774), *German.*

GAINSBOROUGH, Thomas (1727-1788), *English.*

GOYA, Francisco Jose   De Goya Y Lucientes. (1746-1828), *Spanish.*

DAVID, Jacques-Louis (1748-1825), *French.*

BLAKE, William (1757-1827), *English.*

TURNER, Joseph Mallord William (1775-1851), *English.*

INGRES, Jean-Auguste-Dominique (1780-1867) *French.*

GERICAULT, Jean Louis André Théodore (1791-1824), *French.*

DELACROIX, Ferdinand Victor Eugéne (1798-1863), *French.*

DAUMIER, Honoré (1808-1879), *French.*

MANET, Edouard (1832-1883), French.

MILLET, Jean François (1814-1875), *French.*

FUSELI, Henry (1741-1825), *Swiss.*

WHISTLER, James Abbott McNeill (1834-1903), *American.*

RODIN, Auguste (1840-1917), *French.*

DEGAS, Hilaire Germain Edgard (1834-1917), *French.*

CEZANNE, Paul (1839-1906), *French.*

MONET, Claude (1840-1926), *French.*

RENOIR, Pierre Auguste (1841-1919), *French.*

ROUSSEAU, Henri (1844-1910), *French.*

GAUGUIN, Paul (1848-1903), *French.*

VAN GOGH, Vincent (1853-1890), *Dutch.*

SEURAT, Georges (1859-1891), *French.*

MUNCH, Edvard (1863-1944), *Norwegian.*

TOULOUSE-LAUTREC, Henri de (1864-1901), *French.*

KANDINSKY, Wassily (1866-1944), *Russian.*

BEARDSLEY, Aubrey (1872-1898), *English.*

MONDRIAN, Piet (1872-1944), *Dutch.*

THOMSON, Tom (1877-1917), *Canadian*

KLEE, Paul (1979-1940), *Swiss.*

PICASSO, Pablo (1881-1973), *Spanish.*

BRAQUE, Georges (1882-1963), *French.*

DUCHAMP, Marcel (1887-1968), *French.*

O'KEEFFE, Georgia (1887-   ), *American.*

CHAGALL, Marc (1889-1985), *French.*

WOOD, Grant (1892-1942), *American.*

CALDER, Alexander (1898), *American.*

ESCHER, Maurits Cornelis (1898-1972), *Dutch.*

MOORE, Henry (1898-   ), *English.*

MAGRITTE, René (1898-1967), *French.*

ROTHKO, Mark (1903-1970), *Russian born/American.*

DALI, Salvador (1904-   ), *Spanish.*

de KOONING, Willem (1904-   ), *Dutch born/American.*

KLINE, Franz (1910-1962), *American.*

POLLOCK, Jackson (1912-1956), *American.*

COLVILLE, Alex (1920-   ), *Canadian.*

OLDENBURG, Claes (1929-   ), *American.*

WARHOL, Andy (1930-   ), *American.*

BATEMAN, Robert (1930-   ), *Canadian.*

RIOPELLE, Jean-Paul (1923-   ). *Canadian born/French.*

CHRISTO, Christo Javachef (1935-   ), *Bulgarian born/American.*

DANBY, Ken (1940-   ), *Canadian.*

UNGER, Jim (1943-   ), *British born/Canadian.*

BILLY (1977-1985), *Canadian.*